MY FIRST
BIRD BOOK AND BIRD FEEDER

Written and Illustrated by Sharon Lovejoy

WORKMAN PUBLISHING · NEW YORK

Text and illustrations copyright © 2012 by Sharon Lovejoy

Design copyright © Workman Publishing Company, Inc.

Library of Congress Cataloging-in-Publication Data is available.

ISBN 978-0-7611-6599-6

Design by Raquel Jaramillo and Orlando Adiao

Workman books are available at special discounts when purchased in bulk for premiums
and sales promotions as well as for fund-raising or educational use. Special editions or
book excerpts also can be created to specification. For details, contact the Special Sales
Director at the address below, or send an e-mail to specialmarkets@workman.com.

Workman Publishing Company, Inc.
225 Varick Street
New York, NY 10014-4381
www.workman.com

Printed in China

First printing September 2012
10 9 8 7 6 5 4 3 2 1

Watching birds makes every day of my life exciting. Although I have traveled the country and birded in national parks and wildlife refuges, for me the happiest times are in my own backyard.

My wish for you is that you get to know the birds in your yard; they'll make your life more exciting too. You'll be able to enjoy them as they defend their territories, choose mates, build nests, raise their young, feed, take baths, play, and make some of the most beautiful music in the world.

Sharon Lovejoy

San Luis Obispo, California, and South Bristol, Maine

Dedicated to

Sara   Asher   Moses   Ilyahna

CONTENTS

Remember how you felt on the first day of school when you didn't know anyone? You saw new faces and heard new voices and wondered how you'd ever remember so many people and so many names.

But after a few days, somebody spoke, and without even looking up, you knew who was talking. Soon you not only recognized faces and voices but also connected them to names and personalities.

Getting to know the birds who visit your yard and bird feeder is as easy as meeting a new group of kids. All you need to do is exactly what you did with the kids in your school—watch and listen.

Learning about birds is like exploring a new and magical world that is hidden in plain sight. The more time you spend watching them, the more you'll discover. From the clues in this book, you'll learn the names of the little bird who spirals down a tree trunk upside down, and the big, brown bird poking its long bill into an anthill, and why the hummingbird carries bits of spiderweb in its long bill.

Before long, you'll recognize the bird's voices and call them by name. The birds will become, just like the kids in school, good friends.

YOUR BIRD FEEDER

My favorite feeder is the one that comes with your book. Just attach the feeder to a window that you can visit often, like near the kitchen table. You don't need hiking boots or binoculars to watch the birds because they'll be right in front of you, just inches away. If you sit quietly, they'll ignore you, and you can get a close view of their activities.

Sometimes the bigger and more aggressive birds, like jays, will scare away the little birds, but often the little ones just move over and let the jays have their fill. And sometimes, a bossy little bird, like a wren, half the size of a jay, will fly in and take over.

You'll be so close to the birds that you will be able to see the color of their

HOW TO CALL A BIRD

Birds are as curious about you as you are about them. To call them in for closer viewing, softly whisper "pish, pish, pish" or give the back of your hand some kisses. If a bird is building a nest, sitting on a nest, or caring for its young, please don't distract it by calling; be as quiet as a spider.

Be sure to place the feeder in an area away from bushes where a cat might lie in wait, but near trees where a bird can retreat and hide if it feels threatened.

If it takes a while for the birds to find your feeder, place a saucer of water or a birdbath nearby (see page 40 for making your own birdbath). The birds

feathers and small details such as an eye-ring or wing bars. You'll also be able to watch how they behave. These things are clues that will help you identify the birds who come for meals.

that fly in to drink or bathe will discover the food. Once one bird finds the feeder, others will follow and feast.

You'll get to know the birds at your feeder, and they'll get to know you. Some of them may become tame enough to land near or on you. You'll look forward to their visits through every season, and they'll look forward to you keeping their feeder stocked with treats.

Fill the feeder with some seed (see page 30 for foods birds love) or follow one of the simple recipes for treats starting on page 33. Then sit back, browse through your book, and watch for your first visitors.

HOW TO ASSEMBLE AND CARE FOR YOUR FEEDER

Insert the suction cups through the two small holes on the back of the feeder. Attach the feeder to a window that you can visit often.

Place seeds in all three sections of the tray. If the seed in your feeder becomes wet, soiled, or moldy, wash the tray with warm, soapy water; otherwise, clean the tray weekly. Rinse and dry it thoroughly to keep seeds from spoiling. The front of the tray snaps open for easy cleaning.

BIRD CLUES

When trying to identify a new bird at your feeder, you'll need to look for clues. Often the first thing you notice is your best clue. I've listed some questions for you to ask yourself when looking at the bird. You don't

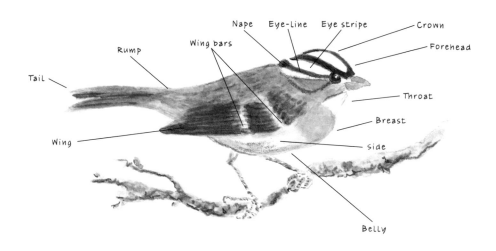

need to answer all of them, but the ones that are easy to answer will help guide you to the right bird. Make a few notes in your journal (page 14) as you watch the bird.

WHAT TO LOOK FOR

Size

How big is the bird? Is it as big as a jay, medium-sized like a sparrow, or tiny like a hummingbird?

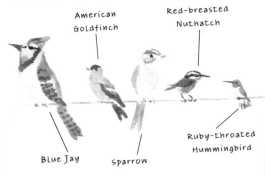

American Goldfinch

Red-breasted Nuthatch

Blue Jay

Sparrow

Ruby-throated Hummingbird

Shape

Is the bird tall, short, fat, or skinny? Sometimes birds will fluff up during cold weather, so on a chilly day they can look almost twice as big as their real size.

This plump Black-capped Chickadee is fluffed up for warmth.

Color

What color are the feathers? Are there any bars, streaks, patches, or spots?

Red-shafted Flicker feather

Head

What's the shape of the bill? Is it cone-shaped, long and needlelike? Or curved down, or thick and heavy? Are the eyes brightly colored? Do you see any eye-rings? Does the bird have a crest of feathers on its head?

Yellowthroats have a long, needlelike bill.

Flight

Does the bird hover like a helicopter or fly in a straight line? Does it dip up and down

as it flies? Does it fly low to the ground from bush to bush, or flit, secretively, from branch to branch high in the treetops?

Watch how Bluebirds will drop to the ground to catch insects.

Feet

What color are the legs and feet? Look at how the toes are arranged. Are there two toes in front and two in back, or three in front and one in back?

American Robin's foot

Tail

Is the tail long, short, narrow, or wide? Does it stand straight up? How is the tail shaped? Here are some common shapes:

Fan   Forked   Notched

Squared   Rounded   Pointed

Behavior and Habits

Watch how the bird acts. Does it use its feet to kick up leaves and twigs? Does it pump its tail up and down? Do you see it clinging to a tree and hammering the bark with its bill? Does it walk or hop? Does it perch and sing in the same spot every day?

The Eastern Towhee
kicks up leaves and twigs.

LISTEN FOR BIRD WORDS

Every bird has its own special call. Listen! Some birds sound like they are singing real words. Here are my favorites:

🐦 Barred Owl: "Who cooks for you? Who cooks for you all?"

🐦 Red-eyed Vireo: "Look up! See me: Over here, this way. Do you hear me? Higher still, chewy!"

🐦 Chestnut-sided Warbler: "Very, very pleased to meetcha!"

🐦 Eastern Meadowlark: "Spring of the year! See you, soon. I will see you. Spring is here!"

KEEP A BIRD JOURNAL

Record the birds who visit your feeder in a bird journal. You can use a small notebook or you can make your own bird-shaped journal (see page 17). Keep the journal near where you watch the feeder and write notes about the birds you see in your yard. You can also draw pictures or snap a quick photo with a digital camera. Glue the pictures into your journal along with the date you saw the bird.

When you spot a bird you don't know, grab your journal and watch quietly. Write down your visitor's most noticeable features and note special marks, like tail patches or spots. After the bird flies away, you can then leaf through the Bird Guide (see page 48) to find the bird and read more about it.

The notes you take in your journal will help you understand the secret lives of the birds—their yearly

feb 22.
Warm today
Lots of Jays & Goldfinches at my feeder.

I counted 14!
They talk a lot and eat a lot. The wren came back!

patterns of migration, where they like to nest, the time of day they come to eat, and how they are influenced by weather, other birds, and the seasons. Here are some things to write down:

🐦 The date, the time, and what you see. Some birds will always appear early in the day to feed, others later in the afternoon. Note where the bird was found, for instance, in a hedge, an apple tree, or in your feeder. (You can use the map of your yard for this. See page 43.)

🐦 How is the weather? Cold, sunny, rainy, windy? Do you notice the birds eating more when the weather changes, or when certain plants are in season, or when a lot of moths or bugs appear?

🐦 Can you see which foods the birds eat? This will help you decide what to put in your feeder. Maybe the birds are kicking out most of the seeds and eating only one kind.

🐦 Are there young birds visiting or sitting nearby and waiting for a parent to bring food? What are

15

the parents feeding their young?

🐚 Do any of the birds act like bullies at your feeder?

🐚 Do you notice that some birds have left for the season while other new visitors have arrived? Identify the birds and use your journal to keep track of when they arrive and leave.

When you keep a journal with dates, you'll be able to look back and predict when different species of birds will arrive in the spring or leave on their annual migration. You'll learn what they like to eat, when and where they nest, and the way they fly or behave.

COMING AND GOING

As you become friends with the birds, you'll notice that some are with you all year, but others may come in the spring and leave in the fall. When it gets tough for birds to find a supply of food, some will migrate (move) to a different location, sometimes flying thousands of miles.

BIRD-SHAPED JOURNAL

Make your own simple bird-shaped journal out of colorful paper. You'll need:

- One piece of heavy paper for the pattern outline
- Bristol board, which is heavier than construction paper, for the cover
- 7 or 8 sheets of colored construction paper
- Scissors
- Hole punch
- One brass round-head fastener to hold the paper together

1. Draw a simple bird outline on heavy paper and cut it out. This will be your pattern.

2. Trace the bird pattern onto two sheets of bristol board. These will be the journal's front and back covers. Cut out the covers.

3. Trace the bird pattern onto the sheets of colored construction paper and cut out the shapes.

4. Stack the bird shapes and use a hole punch to make an eye hole.

5. Fasten the covers and pages together by inserting a brass fastener through the eye holes.

6. Fan out the book. Now you're ready to write your bird notes on the pages.

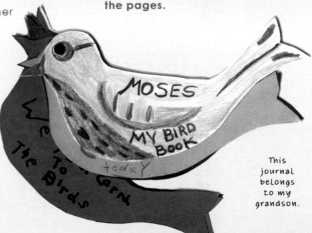

MOSES

MY BIRD BOOK

We To Corn The Birds

today

This journal belongs to my grandson.

FEATHERS

What makes birds like nothing else on the planet? They can fly, but so can bats and insects. Only birds have feathers!

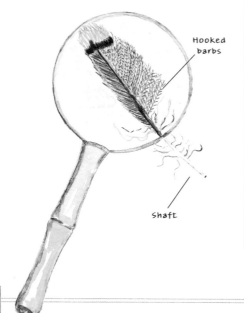

Hooked barbs

Shaft

A feather is a letter from a bird and each kind of feather tells its own story. They come in many shapes, sizes, colors, and textures. Some are for showing off when a male is trying to impress a female, and others are for camouflage (or hiding). Some are for warmth or waterproofing. Some act as tail props to help a bird hold on to a tree; others make sounds or help a bird do fancy, speed flying.

Here's a little detective work for you: If you find a feather, use a magnifying glass to look at its hooked barbs. Ruffle the feather by running your finger from the top of the feather to the bottom of the shaft. Now pinch the feather between your fingers and run your fingers the other way. See how the feather zips back together when the tiny, hooked barbs reconnect? Sleek feathers (like the ones you just smoothed down) make it easier for a bird to fly and to stay warm and dry.

Contour Feathers

Shinglelike layers of contour feathers cover a bird's body, give it color and shape, protect it from sunburn (yes, birds can get sunburned!), and shed water like a raincoat.

Down Feathers

Fluffy down feathers, hidden under the contour feathers, hold air next to the skin to keep the bird warm, just like when you snuggle in a down-filled sleeping bag or down jacket.

Flight Feathers

One side of this flight feather is wide and the other narrow. The narrow side, called the leading edge, always faces the direction the bird is flying. Its knifelike shape makes it easier for the feather to slice through the air.

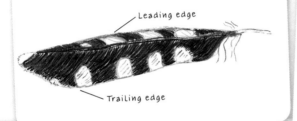

Leading edge

Trailing edge

Filoplumes

These stiff hairlike feathers with barbed tips are attached to nerve endings. Filoplumes send information to the bird about many things, including where to position their other feathers for easier flying.

Tail Feathers

See how both edges of these tail feathers are the same? Flying birds can make their tail feathers open, close, and lift to help them steer, change directions quickly, and rise on air currents. These feathers also act as brakes, slowing down flight.

Afterfeathers

Afterfeathers are small feathers attached to the side of contour feathers. Afterfeathers give a bird an extra layer of insulation.

Dirty Birds

Healthy birds need clean feathers. When you see a bird tugging at a feather and pulling it through its bill, the bird is preening. Birds use their bills to spread a waxy oil from the preen oil gland onto each feather a few times a day to keep them waterproof and flexible.

Birds take dry baths with dirt and dust. They sit in dirt and fling it over themselves, just the way they do when they're in water. This is their way to clean off parasites and extra preen oil.

You can put a big plant saucer or a garbage can lid in an open, sunny spot, and fill it with loose soil. Watch how the birds take a dirt bath and then comb their feathers.

HAIR TO HORNS

What do your hair and fingernails, a rhinoceros's horn, and an alligator's claws have in common with a bird's feathers? All four are made from a strong, lightweight material called keratin.

TALONS AND TOES

Bird feet work double duty; they're used as both hands *and* feet. Birds use their feet to hold food, to play, to eat, and to hold and use tools just like you use your hands. By looking closely at a bird's toes, you'll soon be able to tell if the bird you're watching is a tree climber or if it spends most of its life on the ground or perched in a tree. The sharp and powerful talons (toes) of birds of prey, like hawks, eagles, and owls, are used as weapons. Once they grab a small bird, rodent, or snake, it seldom escapes.

Perching Bird Toes

Like most birds at your feeder, perching birds have three toes in front and a long back toe, which helps them grip and keep their balance. Ground-feeding birds have a short rear toe.

Woodpecker Toes

The little Downy Woodpecker has two toes in front and two in back that are perfect for clinging to and climbing the bark of a tree.

Autolock Toes

Why don't birds fall off a perch when they sleep? Because they have two thin tendons in the backs of their legs that automatically lock their toes around a branch when they sit or sleep.

Owl Talons

Owls' toes are called talons. An owl's outside front toe, called an opposable toe, can turn backward until it meets the hind toe. Just like your thumb, which allows you to pick up and hold things securely, the owl's opposable toe helps it to grab and hold its prey.

Recognize this? It's Mother Nature's all-purpose human foot with five toes instead of a bird's four. What can your toes do?

BILLS AND BEAKS

The shape of a bird's bill will give you clues about what that bird eats. Birds with bills can pluck fruit, grab insects from the air, tug worms from the ground, hammer into wood in search of insects, and sip nectar from a flower and sap from a tree. Birds with beaks can rip flesh into small pieces. Bills and beaks can also gather twigs and build nests. Some birds use them to make music, clacking and clattering them like a drum. And sometimes birds use their bills as tools and weapons.

Bewick's Wren

Big and All-Purpose

A big, all-purpose bill, like on this jay, is perfect for cracking nuts, grabbing and eating insects, lizards, snakes, eggs, and small birds.

Blue Jay

Long and Thin

The long, thin bill of a hummingbird can dip deep inside a tube-shaped flower so the hummer can lap its nectar with its tubular, fringed tongue. Hummingbirds also use their needlelike bills to catch small insects, pluck spiders out of webs, and drink sweet sap running from a tree.

Ruby-throated Hummingbird

Thick and Strong

The thick, strong bill of the woodpecker is perfect for hammering and chiseling wood. Watch the chips fly as it makes a nesting hole or chisels tunnels in search of insects.

Hairy Woodpecker

Cone-Shaped

The cone-shaped bill, like this cardinal's, is hefty and powerful for cracking nuts and seeds.

Northern Cardinal

Tweezerlike

The long, thin, tweezerlike bill of insect-eating birds, like this little Red-eyed Vireo, pokes in leaves and bark in search of hidden food.

Red-eyed Vireo

Strong, Hooked Beaks

The strong, hooked beaks of owls, eagles, falcons, and hawks tell the story of a flesh-tearing bird. You won't find any of these birds of prey in this Bird Guide, but you never know when you'll find one outdoors. The Barred Owl, a fierce nighttime hunter, flies to a perch with prey in its talons and rips it into small pieces with its beak.

Barred Owl

STRONG AS NAILS

A bird's bill gets worn and chipped just like your fingernails, and just like your fingernails, the bill grows slowly over time.

The powerful, big beak of the Golden Eagle is strong enough to rip apart prey as large as seals and mountain goats, but mostly the eagle uses its beak to tear apart rabbits, reptiles, gamebirds, and other small animals. The Golden Eagle will also use its beak to fight off animals who try to steal its prey.

The thick, curved, upper beak of the little falcon called an American Kestrel has a "tooth," which juts down like a can opener. This "tooth" fits into a notch on the lower part of the beak. Though the kestrel's beak is small, it is mighty and can snap a spinal cord in half.

Golden Eagle

American Kestrel

CROP AND GIZZARD

You have thirty-two teeth and a jaw strong enough to chew meat, grind up peanuts, and munch on carrots and celery. Birds don't have *any* teeth, so how do they chew their food?

A bird picks up grit from the ground and passes the tiny rocks, sand, and gravel through its body into its tough, muscular stomach, which is also called a gizzard. The powerful walls of the gizzard (much more fun to

say than stomach) contract and expand to push and smash the food against the grit until it is ground up like the food you chew.

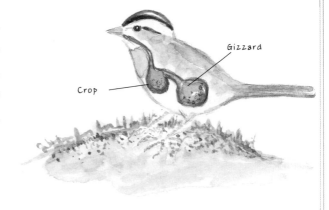

Don't You Wish You Had a Crop?

Most birds have a small pouch (some have two) called a crop, where they can store food to eat later. (It's like a "doggie bag" of leftovers you take home from a restaurant.) If a bird flies over a patch of yummy-looking sunflowers filled with seeds, it will swoop down and stuff its gizzard. When the gizzard is full, it will cram more food into its baglike crop until the crop is as full as your school backpack.

When the bird can't swallow another bite of food, it will fly to a safe perch and slowly begin to digest what is in its gizzard. As the gizzard empties, the food in the crop, which has been moistened and softened, will make its way to the gizzard for grinding and digesting.

FOOD FOR THE BIRDS

Has anyone ever told you that you "eat like a bird"? You'll have to explain that couldn't possibly be true because some birds can eat more than their body weight in food every day. Can you imagine eating more than what you weigh? Food is birds' fuel; it gives them strength, the energy to fly long distances, and helps keep them warm.

Birds can eat packaged seed mixes or some of the Top Ten Seeds (page 32), but they also enjoy the foods we eat. In the Seasonal Treats section (page 33) you'll find recipes you can make with foods from your garden, cupboard, or fridge.

Many grocery, hardware, and feed stores offer bags of wild songbird seed mix. Look for mixes that include white proso millet, black sunflower

FUEL FOR WINTER

A bird who stuffs its crop and gizzard with food is more likely to survive a freezing winter night. As the bird snoozes, its body slowly digests the food, which helps keep it warm.

seed, and cracked corn because all of these appeal to a variety of birds. You can vary your bird feeder offerings by adding small pieces of fruit, peanuts (a special treat for jays, chickadees, and nuthatches), and crushed eggshell. Some people feed birds doughnuts and bread, which is like a junk-food diet. It fills

This happy scarecrow welcomes hungry birds.

birds up, but doesn't provide them with the nutrients they need to survive.

Not all the birds you invite to your feeder like what's in the store-bought mixed seed. Some are picky eaters and they'll ignore your feeder or choose only the seeds they like. In the process of picking and scratching through the mix, much of it will be kicked out of the feeder. Usually they are looking for one or more of the goodies in the Top Ten list below. They are bird-tested and proven winners.

TOP TEN SEEDS AND FEEDS FOR YOUR FEEDER

1. Black oil sunflower seed is rich, oily, and easy for birds to crack open.

2. Millet attracts birds not normally interested in feeders. Mockingbirds, catbirds, thrashers, thrushes, wrens, cardinals, and bluebirds will stop by for a snack.

3. Gray-striped sunflower seed

4. White proso millet

5. Cracked corn

6. Chicken grit includes crushed oyster shell, which gives the birds calcium and minerals. This grit is especially great in winter when birds can't find sand and pebbles under the snow.

7. Thistle seed is also called nyjer or black nyjer. Goldfinches love this!

8. Raw peanuts in the shell are a favorite of jays, chickadees, and nuthatches. The jays will stuff themselves, then hide some for future snacking.

9. Safflower seed is a good one to use if you're bothered by starlings, grackles, and squirrels, who will not eat it. Cardinals love it.

10. Milo (aka sorghum) is loved by doves.

SEASONAL TREATS FOR THE TWEETS

Just as you might like to eat a hot bowl of soup in the winter and cool Popsicles in the summer, birds also like to eat different treats throughout the year.

This snowman is dressed with apple cores and other treats for the birds.

Winter

In the winter, offer your birds a treat of sunflower hearts, which are shelled sunflower seeds. Birds have easy access to the hearts and don't have to use their energy to crack open the sunflower's tough hulls.

Bird Booster

Peanut butter isn't just *your* favorite; the birds love it and need it during cold weather. The Bird Booster not only tastes good, but will give birds fat and protein to help them through the cold weather.

- 1½ cups peanut butter
  (low-cost is okay)
- 1½ cups shortening, bacon
  grease, suet, or all three mixed
  together
- 3 cups yellow cornmeal
- 1 cup flour
- 1 cup sand

Mix all ingredients until thoroughly blended. Smear it into a pinecone or on a tree trunk.

Save Your Apple Cores

Don't toss that apple core! What birds love most about apples is the inner core—the part you don't eat. Save some cores, string them on wire, and hang from a clothesline or branch. Sit back and watch the birds flock in to feed.

Spring

Welcome your songsters and bluebirds back to your yard with these tasty spring treats.

Songbird Mush

- 1 cup raisin bran cereal crushed
  with rolling pin
- ½ cup berries (dried or fresh)

1½ cups bacon grease or suet

½ cup sand

Mix these together thoroughly and pack the goo into a pinecone or a small log drilled with holes. Hang it in a cool dry area away from bushes where cats may lurk. Or serve it in a bowl, half a coconut, half an orange, or a plant saucer.

Hummingbird Syrup

If Hummingbirds are in your yard year-round, this delicious drink can be offered in every season. In areas with severe winters, fill your feeder with syrup from spring through late September. Sometimes

YUMMY SUET

Suet is a dense, high-energy food that birds crave and need in their diet, especially during early spring, fall, and winter. You can tuck the hard cake into an inexpensive wire suet basket that can be bought at hardware, feed, or bird supply stores. Hang the basket from a branch near your feeder. Suet attracts insect-eating birds such as chickadees, titmice, nuthatches, wrens, woodpeckers, sapsuckers, warblers, creepers, mockingbirds, orioles, jays, and cardinals.

hummers arrive before flowers bloom, so this is a welcome

and lifesaving drink. Keep the feeders out until late September to help migrating hummers or birds who are knocked off course during storms.

SPECIAL TREATS

Tubular red flowers are hummingbird favorites. If you have fuchsia, sage, lavender, nasturtium, columbine, or trumpet vine in your yard, the hummingbirds are probably already visitors. Or, provide them with a hummingbird feeder and fill it with homemade syrup (see the recipe on this page). Feed the hummingbirds, and they'll stay with you for months. You can buy a hummingbird feeder at a pet, hardware, or wild bird store.

¼ cup granulated sugar (Never use honey or food coloring!)

1 cup water

Mix the sugar and the water in a small, microwavable mixing bowl. Microwave on high for about a minute and a half. Stir again, making sure that all the sugar has dissolved. Allow to cool, then fill the feeder and hang it in a sheltered area (direct sun will cause the sugared water to ferment).

Be sure to clean out the feeder at least every three days with hot water and soap. Use a bottle brush or toothbrush. Rinse thoroughly.

Summer

Orioles and tanagers, the most colorful of summer garden birds, love the taste of oranges. With the help of a grown-up, hammer some nails into a board or post. Slice oranges in half and push them onto the nails.

You'll find that almost any fruit you love is a favorite of birds too. Put blueberries and pieces of strawberries, peaches, grapes, or cherries in your bird feeder and watch who comes to visit. You may be surprised by the dazzle of a golden oriole or the flash of a bluebird's wings.

Fall

The big, bright sunflower makes a delicious autumn bird snack. Cut whole sunflower heads and place them on your feeder. Or you can have a grown-up help you cut out the center of the head to make a simple bird-feeder wreath to hang on a fence or post.

SOS–Save Our Seeds

After carving your Halloween pumpkin, save the seeds for the birds. Just throw out the gooey innards and spread the seeds out to dry. The birds (and squirrels) will thank you!

SPLAT!
THE STORY OF BIRD POOP

Watch what the birds at your feeder and in your yard eat. Whatever a bird eats turns into poop. You'll see traces of their meals splattered, splashed, whitewashed, and polka-dotted all over sidewalks and cars, and beneath where the birds sit or sleep. Some poops are as purple as grapes, some red as paint, some inky black, and others black and white or green and white. The colors depend on what the bird eats. If a bird eats red berries . . . well, you'll be able to tell by its poop. When birds eat and digest their food, sometimes whole seeds are deposited in their droppings. The seeds help replant meadows, forests, fruits, and flowers.

Thank you, birds!

The polka-dot splatters were left by a flock of Cedar Waxwings who ate a meal of red pyracantha berries.

Mockingbirds who eat the petals of fruit blossoms or fruit may have poop that is a muddy green with a chalky tip of white, which is dried pee.

A crow who eats a mixed diet of lizards, worms, seeds, and corn will leave a thick coil of black poop topped with dried, white pee.

The robin who left this must have gorged herself on purple elderberries, because her poop is purple-blue.

Goldfinches flock to feeders filled with black nyjer seed. You can see bits of nyjer in their poop and pee.

A jay who ate a mixed diet of peanuts, fruit, eggs, and reptiles left this poop.

Surprise! This may look like bird poop, but it is a Pearly Wood Nymph moth in disguise. Birds, who love to eat moths, ignore this moth because of its great camouflage.

MAKE A BIRD HAVEN

What will make the birds not only drop in to feed, but also hang around, sleep, and raise their young? It's simple: food, water, and shelter—plus a little help from you.

Splish-Splash, Make a Birdbath

Creating a small birdbath can be very simple. Dig a shallow hole in the ground and sink a large waterproof saucer or garbage can lid, or line the hole with a rubber pond-liner. Fill

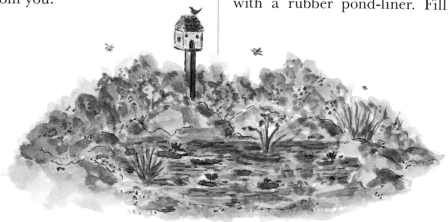

the hole or container with water and set some stones in the center for a bird perch.

Make a Lifesaving Shelter

Start by laying a few thick branches on the ground and then cross-layer with twigs, leafy branches, more twigs, and more branches. Birds will scoot inside your shelter for safety and will sleep there on cold nights.

SOCK IT TO 'EM

In the spring, birds will welcome your offerings of fibers and twigs for their nests. Stuff a holey sock with grasses and finger-length strings, or make a "nesting supply tree" and dangle fibers from its branches.

Grow Food

If you want to grow one super-power flower to attract birds, make it a sunflower. In the spring, plant sunflower seeds in a large pot or plot of ground. Water when dry. When the sunflowers blossom in late August through October,

Birds love the tasty sunflower seeds.

Even one berry bush will attract birds.

you'll be surprised by how many birds will feed on the heavy, seed-filled heads. (See page 37 for some ways to make sunflower seeds extra-delicious.)

Make a Yard Map

Draw the area around your bird feeder and make a map of your yard. Mark an X where your feeder is mounted; sketch in bushes and trees. Note on your map where you've seen birds hiding, eating, or nesting.

If you have evergreen trees or berry bushes in your yard, you're lucky because birds can find shelter and food there all year long.

Your backyard map will show you where to place feeders, birdbaths, and birdhouses.

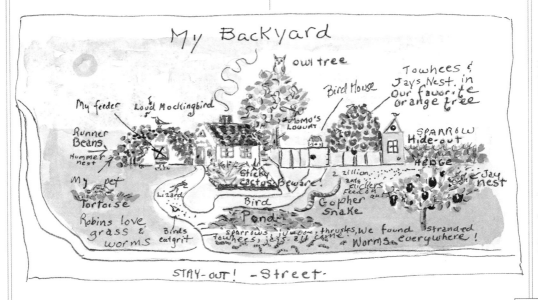

My Backyard

owl tree

Bird House

Towhees & Jays Nest in Our favorite orange tree

My feeder   Loud Mockingbird

Momo's Lookout

SPARROW Hide-out

Runner Beans

Hummer nest

HEDGE

Jay nest

My pet Tortoise

Lizard

Sticky cactus Beware!

2 zillion ants suckers feed on

Robins love grass & worms

Birds eat grit

Bird Pond

Gopher Snake

sparrows, juncos, thrushes, We found stranded towhees, jays all came Worms everywhere!

STAY-OUT! -Street-

Birds don't always nest in trees, bushes, and vines; sometimes they find other kinds of homes and nest in the strangest places.

Woodpeckers usually make their own hole-homes in trees, chiseling and chipping until

it is just right for them. The Downy Woodpecker (left) was fooled by the bark on this birdhouse, which made it look like a tree. He made the hole bigger and settled in to raise a family.

Wrens nest in sheds and tree holes and on porches, patios, and decks. They are brave and bossy little birds and will watch you with their bright eyes, chitter and scold, but go right on with the business of laying eggs and tending their young, even in an old hat!

The Carolina Wren on the next page flew right in the open

door of a garden shed and made her nest in an old tea kettle. She sometimes lines her nest with the cast-off skins of snakes, who shed them as they grow.

Chickadees nest in tree holes, but they'll also move into little birdhouses. They'll investigate thoroughly, then set out to make them comfy by lining the insides with hair, fur, moss, feathers, and the cocoons of moths.

When you clean out your hairbrush or comb, put some strands of your hair on a branch. In a few days you might see your hair woven into a bird's nest!

BUG HUNTERS

Nesting birds gather hundreds of caterpillars and insects a day to feed their hungry young. They are your garden's all-natural pest control team.

45

MAKE YOUR OWN FEEDERS

The more kinds of feeders and foods you offer, the more kinds of birds will visit your yard and your window feeder.

Some birds like to eat from tables, just like you. Other birds like to feed from tree stumps or from simple platforms raised high above the ground. Tiny birds will visit small, hanging feeders, like coconut and orange halves. Try some of these feeders:

A dead tree or branch stuck securely in the ground or in a big container filled with soil or rocks makes a fast-food restaurant for many kinds of birds. Nail a metal collar about twenty-four inches up the tree branch to keep squirrels and raccoons from stealing food.

Make a "bluebird table" out of a piece of wood nailed to a post or set on a rock. Offer raisins, chopped peanuts, or dried or fresh fruits.

🌰 Offer ground-feeding birds, like Mourning Doves, juncos, and sparrows, a simple saucer filled with seed.

🌰 Pick the fruit out of a half grapefruit or orange. Leave the empty peel on a windowsill for a couple of days and until it's dry and hard. Poke three holes in the side of the dried fruit skin for a hanger, fill with seed, and hang from a tree branch. Small birds flock to these feeders.

🌰 Top a feeding post with a salt block to lure in many different birds who need salt in their diets.

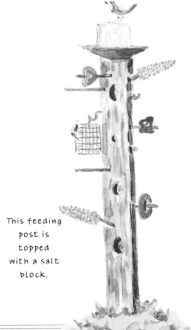

This feeding post is topped with a salt block.

THE BIRD GUIDE

Almost all the birds featured in this book are songbirds that you may see eating at your window feeder. Although there are more than 700 species of birds in North America, they won't all come to visit you. Mostly you'll have some seed-, nut-, and fruit-eating birds, like goldfinches, nuthatches, chickadees, sparrows, and finches.

I've also included a few regular backyard visitors, like Mourning Doves, towhees, juncos, sparrows, and Northern Flickers, who prefer to eat the seeds that spill on the ground from the feeder. Then there are the hangers-on, woodpeckers, who will swoop in, prop themselves against the side of the feeder with their stiff tail feathers, and stuff themselves on peanuts and seeds.

HOME, HOME ON THE RANGE

Always check the little range map at the bottom of each bird's page. The map will show you if that bird lives in your area.

The profiles are arranged so that birds who share some similar features are grouped together. This way, if you spot a bird with a big, thick bill, you can leaf through the book until you find a few birds with the same feature. Once you've narrowed down your choices, it will be easier for you to identify the bird at your feeder.

MOURNING DOVE

Large body, about 12 inches long

Small head

Long, thin tail

Full chest

White tips on outer tail feathers (visible when in flight)

Black spots on sides of neck and wings

RANGE: Found almost everywhere in the United States except heavy forests. Doves feed on the ground and on platform, shelf, and table feeders.

OTHER BIRDS TILT THEIR HEADS BACK TO SWALLOW, BUT A MOURNING DOVE SUCKS WATER THROUGH ITS BILL LIKE A STRAW.

Mourning Doves get their name from the quiet, sad song they coo over and over. Male and females bond (pair off), and the female lays two eggs in a messy, open nest of twigs. Both birds take turns sitting on the eggs to keep them warm; the male takes the day shift and the female takes the night. Twelve to fourteen days later, the eggs will hatch. Both parents will feed their young even after they leave the nest.

LISTEN FOR: A slow "coo-uh-coo, coo, coo." Also listen for the whistle or whinnying noise of a Mourning Dove when it takes flight. Males also use their wing noises to attract females.

BIRD MILK: To feed their young, Mourning Doves (and some other birds) produce "milk" in their crop (see page 29). The baby bird sticks its head down the throat of the parent, who regurgitates, or brings up, the rich "milk" into the baby bird's mouth.

RUBY-THROATED HUMMINGBIRD

Small, black chin

Brilliant red throat

Metallic green back

Grayish-white chest

Small body, about 3¼ inches long

Forked, dark green tail

RANGE: From the eastern United States to the Midwest and Canada, and south to the Gulf Coast. Found in parks, gardens, orchards, and deciduous woodlands.

A HUMMINGBIRD'S NEST IS VERY SMALL— ABOUT THE SIZE OF A MARSHMALLOW.

Zip, zip, zip, the fast wing beats, almost seventy-five per second, announce the arrival of this tiny flying jewel. Watch these masters of fancy flight dart between flowers to sip nectar, which is their high-powered fuel.

They'll sip sweet sap from tree trunks and pluck spiders from webs. The female will use the spider silk to build their nests. If you're lucky, you can see her using her long tongue to lick and glue the spider silk into the cup-shaped nest.

LISTEN FOR: A chittery, repetitious "chit, chit, chit," "chee it, chee it, chee it," or "did, did, did, did, did," along with the loud humming and slapping of wings.

LOOK FOR: The female has a white chin and throat. Her body is dully colored with a shining golden-green back and has a fan-shaped tail with white-tipped outer feathers.

The female tends to her chicks.

ANNA'S HUMMINGBIRD

MALE

Rosy-red throat,
sides of neck,
and forehead

White behind eye

Small body, about
4 inches long

Green back

Broad, slightly
notched
gray-edged tail

FEMALE

Patch of
red flecks
under chin

Grayish-green

Green-gray spots on the chest

Rounded green tail with white tips

RANGE: From the West Coast to Canada and Alaska, and south into Mexico. Found in parks, gardens, orchards, deciduous woodlands, deserts, chaparral, and coastal sage scrub.

HUMMERS BUILD TINY NESTS OF MOSSES, LICHENS, SPIDERWEBS, FIBERS, AND FEATHERS.

These gabby hummingbirds, with their tiny, squeaky call, welcome the sunrise with their endless songs. Nothing in the garden escapes the Anna's attention. They'll watch as feeders are filled, and sometimes land on the feeder before it is hung. The males show off during mating season with a high, arcing flight ending in a fast dive and loud burst of noise from his tail feathers.

LISTEN FOR: "Zeet, zeet, zeet, zeet," "chi, chi, chi, chi, chi," and a scratchy, squeaky "tsee, tsee, tsee, chink-chonk." Trace the sounds and you'll find the hummer perched on a twig or wire.

Mama lays one or two eggs the size of small jelly beans.

Two baby hummers fill the nest. Mama brings food to them all day long.

After about three weeks, the babies sit on the edge of the nest, then helicopter up and fly away.

DOWNY WOODPECKER

Small body, about 5½ to 7 inches long

Blocky head with patch of red on back (males)

Black wings with white spots

White sides, straight white back

Short bill

Two toes facing front, two toes facing back

RANGE: Found throughout the United States, Downies will visit feeders and search trees for insects.

AFTER THE DOWNY LEAVES ITS NESTING HOLE, OTHER BIRDS WILL CROWD INSIDE ON COLD NIGHTS.

The little Downy Woodpecker performs like an acrobat, hanging upside down or hopping—not climbing—up and down trees. He'll poke, tap, and pick, then listen closely to the bark for the sounds of bugs, grubs, and other tasty critters, which he'll quickly snatch with his long, sensitive, barbed tongue.

In the spring, the male Downy will drum on a tree for two weeks as he chisels out a one-and-a-quarter-inch hole for a nest. The sound attracts females looking for a mate.

Female Downy Woodpecker

LISTEN FOR: "Pik, pik, pik," and a laughing, quick rattle that sounds like "treeeeeeee, eeee, eee, eee, eee, ee." You'll also hear quick spurts of "drum, drum, drum, rat, tat, tat"—that's a Downy's bill pounding or hammering at a tree.

SPECIAL TREATS: Lure a Downy into your feeder with sunflower hearts in the summer and suet or Bird Booster mix (see page 33) in the cold winter months.

NORTHERN FLICKER

Large, brown body, about 11 to 12 inches long

Red patch on back of head

Down-curved bill

Brown striped back

Black mustache

Brilliant red or yellow-gold underwings (visible when it flies)

Black bib on chest

Shining white rump patch (visible when it flies)

Underparts speckled with black spots

RANGE: The Yellow-shafted Flicker is found in the East, and the Red-shafted Flicker is found in the West. Widespread in parks, gardens, woodlands, and some deserts.

THERE ARE TWO FORMS OF NORTHERN FLICKERS: YELLOW-SHAFTED FLICKERS AND RED-SHAFTED FLICKERS.

This big relative of wood-peckers is found on the ground more often than in trees. He is called the "anteater bird" for his long tongue (three inches longer than his bill), which resembles the anteater's saliva-sticky, barbed tongue. The sharp dagger at the tip of the flicker's tongue is used to spear fat grubs and bugs. Flickers eat thousands of ants and termites a day.

LISTEN FOR: A loud, piercing "keer, keer, keer" and a repetitive "wick-a, wick-a, wick-a." Its laughing call sounds more like a jungle animal than a bird and earned the flicker the nickname "Wake-Up Bird"!

LOOK FOR: You'll know it's a flicker by its broad, brilliantly colored underwing feathers of yellow or bright reddish-orange.

A male Red-shafted Flicker has a red mustache.

Yellow-shafted Flicker feather

Red-shafted Flicker feather

BLUE JAY

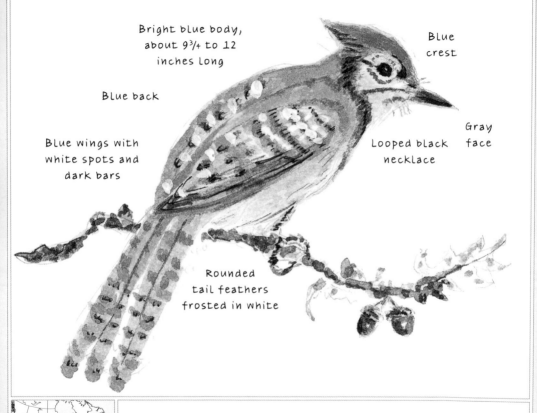

Bright blue body, about 9¾ to 12 inches long

Blue crest

Blue back

Blue wings with white spots and dark bars

Gray face

Looped black necklace

Rounded tail feathers frosted in white

RANGE: Eastern United States, Canada, range extending west and sometimes found in the Northwest. Found in gardens, parks, and mixed woods.

THE OLDEST RECORDED AGE OF A BLUE JAY IS TWENTY-SIX YEARS IN CAPTIVITY AND SEVENTEEN YEARS IN THE WILD. MOST JAYS LIVE ABOUT SEVEN OR EIGHT YEARS.

This brilliant male blue bird is the noisiest member of the feeding party, but when he travels across open spaces or helps his mate feed their young, he's as quiet as falling snow. Watch how he lowers his crest when he feels safe or raises it when he feels threatened and wants to look big and scary. These are smart birds who will remember that you're the one filling the feeder. They may trail after you and chatter as you walk through the yard.

LISTEN FOR: Loud name-calling "jay, jay, jay," "tweedle, tweedle, tweedle," "toodle, toodle," "pedunkle, pedunkle," "dirt, dirt," a sound like a squeaky door, nasal calls, mimicking calls of hawks and other birds, quiet murmuring (especially to their mate and young), and clicking. So many sounds from one bird!

WESTERN SCRUB-JAY

Large body, about 11 to 12 inches long

White eyebrow over dark eye patch

Blue-gray upperparts

Thick, powerful bill

White throat with blue necklace

Pale undersides

LISTEN FOR: Loud, nasal scolding calls, "sweep, sweep, sweep, sweep," "shenk, shenk, shenk," "kuk, kuk."

SPECIAL TREATS FOR THE JAYS: Jays become tame and will beg for food, sometimes even tapping on windows to remind you that it's breakfast time. Watch how a jay carries a whole peanut to a perch, tucks it securely between its feet, and pounds it open with its strong bill.

RANGE: Found in the western United States in oak and pine forests, parks, and gardens.

STELLER'S JAY

White striping on head

Large head topped by a sooty gray triangular crest

White eyebrow

Long, straight dark bill

Dark back

Dark blue wings and tail

Large body, about 12 to 13½ inches long

LISTEN FOR: "Sheck, sheck, sheck, sheck," screeches like a hawk, and sounds mimicking other birds. The male will sing a sweet, quiet murmuring song to his mate.

LOOK FOR: Watch how the Steller's Jay raises his fancy black crest when threatened by other birds. Steller's Jays will hop about on the ground in search of lizards, snakes, and other food.

RANGE: Found in the western United States in gardens, woods, parks, and campgrounds.

AMERICAN CROW

Very large body, about 15³/₄ to 21 inches long

Brown eyes

Black bill

Black feathers look iridescent violet-blue in sunlight.

Wing feathers that spread out like fingers when in flight

Fan-shaped tail

Black feet and legs

RANGE: Widespread. These brainy birds are able to survive almost anywhere.

CROWS ARE SOME OF THE SMARTEST BIRDS IN THE WORLD. THEY HAVE INCREDIBLE MEMORIES AND CAN RECOGNIZE THE FACES OF HUMANS—AND RECALL WHETHER THAT HUMAN WAS KIND OR CRUEL.

A loud group of shiny black crows may include parents, who mate for life, and many generations of their family. These groups will fearlessly attack owls and hawks (their mortal enemies) and shout and squawk until the unwanted bird moves on.

A nesting female will be fed by her family, and if she leaves the nest for a few minutes, one or two of the family members will stand guard. After young birds leave the nest, the patient parents will feed, train, and care for them for months.

LISTEN FOR: Hoarse cawing and shouting, cooing and sweet murmurings to a mate or nestling, rattling like pennies shaking in a can, and sounds like wooden drumsticks clacking together.

ALL IN THE FAMILY: Young crows will stay with their family and help "babysit" new little brothers and sisters.

BLACK-CAPPED CHICKADEE

White cheeks

Short black bill, perfect for plucking insects, eggs, and seeds

Wings edged in frosty white

Small, chunky body, about 5¼ inches long

Light brown on sides and belly

RANGE: Widespread in northern United States into Alaska and western and southern Canada in gardens and mixed and pine woods, and along rivers and creeks.

CHICKADEES GROW EXTRA BRAIN CELLS DURING THE WINTER TO HELP THEM LOCATE THEIR HIDDEN STASHES OF FOOD.

This curious, little chickadee with white cheeks looks like it is dressed in its best black cap and bib. It will chatter constantly with nearby friends, cling upside down on a feeder, slip seeds out one at a time, then fly to a nearby perch to eat. The male and female will work together for about a week chipping out a nesting hole in a tree, or adopting an old nest or bird house. They'll line the hole with animal fur, feathers, spiderweb, or pieces of cocoon before laying eggs. Watch out when the protective female is on her nest; she'll hiss like a snake if you get too close.

LISTEN FOR: The call "chicka-dee-dee-dee-dee-dee" over and over, or a sad sounding "feeeed me, feeeeed me."

LOOK FOR: A chickadee in flight beats, folds, and dips, making it look like it's riding on invisible waves.

The Chestnut-backed Chickadee is found on the West Coast from Oregon up to Alaska.

TUFTED TITMOUSE

Pointed dark tuft and gray upperparts

Small, stout, black bill

Medium-sized body, about 5½ to 6½ inches long

White chest

Small rust-red side patches

Long gray tail

RANGE: Found throughout the eastern and southeastern United States in suburbs, parks, golf courses, and forests.

FORM A FRIENDSHIP WITH A TUFTED TITMOUSE AND YOU'LL HAVE THIS NONMIGRATORY BIRD AT YOUR FEEDER YEAR-ROUND.

These perky little birds are curious, sociable, and brave (they'll pluck fur from a cat for their nest!). A titmouse will investigate you closely if you kiss the back of your hand loudly or make a "pssshing" sound. The males and females look alike, but once a nest is made, you'll be able to tell them apart. Only the female will incubate the eggs.

Watch a titmouse "hunt" with small groups of White-breasted Nuthatches and chickadees.

LISTEN FOR: "Peter, peter, peter, peter." The call of the Oak Titmouse (found on the West Coast) sounds like "chicka, chicka, chicka" and "pretty, pretty, pretty."

HOW'D THE TITMOUSE GET ITS NAME? From an Old Icelandic word *titr*, meaning small, and from Anglo-Saxon *mase*, which means small bird.

The small gray Oak Titmouse also has a tuft.

RED-BREASTED NUTHATCH

Blue-gray back, shoulders, rump, and wings (females are more lightly colored)

Black cap

Black eye-line

White cheeks

Cinnamon-colored chest

Short tail

Small tapered body, about 4½ inches long

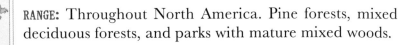

RANGE: Throughout North America. Pine forests, mixed deciduous forests, and parks with mature mixed woods.

NUTHATCHES ARE OFTEN CALLED "TOPSY-TURVY" OR "UPSIDE-DOWN BIRDS" BECAUSE THEY SPEND SO MUCH OF THEIR TIME WORKING THEIR WAY DOWN TREE TRUNKS AND BRANCHES.

The small, thin-billed Red-breasted Nuthatch, whose name came from the word *nuthack*, winds its way headfirst down a tree trunk, picking and poking under bark and into crevices like a detective in search of clues. The Nuthatch is looking for food in crevices and under bark. If it finds something with a tough outer covering, like a beetle or nut, it will wedge the treat securely into the bark and hack it open with its strong bill.

LISTEN FOR: A sound like that of a little car horn—"yank, yank, yank, yank, yank"—repeated many times. The White-breasted Nuthatch (right) call is a nasal "wah, wah, wah, wah."

White-breasted
Nuthatch

MAKE A FRIEND: If these friendly little birds come to your feeder, crack open some nuts, pour them into your hand, and stand still with your hand outstretched. You may have a visitor!

HOUSE WREN

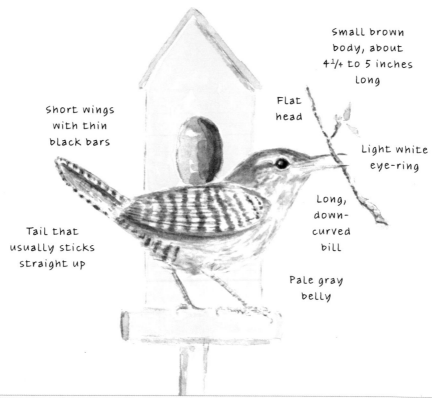

Small brown body, about 4¼ to 5 inches long

Flat head

Short wings with thin black bars

Light white eye-ring

Long, down-curved bill

Tail that usually sticks straight up

Pale gray belly

RANGE: Found throughout North America in suburbs, gardens, farmlands, pastures, parks, golf courses, and hedgerows. Usually nests near houses, which may be how it earned its name.

SOMETIMES THE MALE HOUSE WREN BUSILY BUILDS A DOZEN "DUMMY" NESTS BEFORE THE FEMALE FLIES IN AND CHOOSES ONE TO FINISH.

Even on cloudy days, the sun seems to shine when House Wrens visit your yard. These little birds are curious and bossy, and they'll chase bigger birds away if they get too close to an active nest. Look for wren nests in tree cavities, posts, and birdhouses—even inside a hat, boot, or old work glove.

The male wrens are true homemakers. Although they may return to an old nesting site, they'll take apart the old nest and rebuild it with the same twigs. They are true recyclers.

LISTEN FOR: A song that seems to gurgle and spill from the throat of this active, gabby little bird. You'll hear a churring, scolding, or buzzing sound "chit, chit, chit, chat, chat, chat," a rattle when alarmed, "tsk, tsk, tsk," and the female's call, which sounds like a crying baby.

TINY BIRD: A spunky little House Wren weighs about as much as two nickels.

EASTERN BLUEBIRD

Big, round head

Big eyes with white ring

Royal-blue back on male

Rust-red chest and throat

White belly

Blue wings and tail

Stocky body, 6½ to 8½ inches long

RANGE: From the eastern United States to the eastern foothills of the Rocky Mountains. Found in orchards, gardens, farm fields, meadows, open deciduous woods, and mountain slopes.

BLUEBIRDS FEED ON HIGH-PROTEIN INSECTS WHEN THEY'RE RAISING YOUNG, BUT THEY'LL ALWAYS ENJOY A BERRY FOR DESSERT.

Usually, where there is one bluebird, there will be others. They travel and feed in sociable family flocks and land together in long lines on wires, where they look like bright blue clothespins.

Bluebirds will stop by a feeder to fill up on Songbird Mush (page 34), millet, fruit, and your homemade Bird Booster (page 33). If you have a bluebird box or a tree with a hole in its trunk, they'll use it for nesting or, on cold nights, a family may pile inside for warmth.

LISTEN FOR: Soft, sweet whistles, chittering, "chur, chur, chur, chur," chattering, and "truly, truly, truleeeee." Often calls when flying.

Female Eastern Bluebird has a brownish-gray head.

HOME SWEET HOME: Bluebird houses should be mounted on poles no higher than five feet above the ground and 300 feet apart. This discourages many other birds, who prefer higher nests.

WESTERN BLUEBIRD

Deep blue head, throat, back, wings, and tail

Plump body, about 6½ to 7½ inches long

Chestnut on breast, side, flanks, upper back, and shoulders

Grayish-white belly with a blue wash

RANGE: Found in open pine forests, streamsides, orchards, vineyards, farmlands, mountain slopes, and brushy deserts from the Rocky Mountains to the West Coast.

OTHER BLUEBIRDS WILL BRING FOOD TO THE NEWLY HATCHED BABY BIRDS.

Like their eastern cousins, these small, sky-blue thrushes are often found in large, sociable flocks, but trespassers beware: A male bluebird is a fierce protector of his mate and his nest. He will attack any bluebird who tries to move into his territory, whack it out of the air, wrestle him to the ground, and use his wings as weapons. He'll also do battle with Tree Swallows who might try to take over his nest.

LISTEN FOR: A soft "chit, chit, chit, chit," "cheer, cheer, cheerio," chattering, and whistles.

LOOK FOR: The bright blue flash of the birds as they drop swiftly from a low perch to the ground to nab insects. They'll grab one, then fly to a perch on a post, fenceline, or low growing shrub.

Female
Western Bluebird

AMERICAN ROBIN

Sooty-black head

White eye-ring

Bright yellow bill

Brownish-gray upperparts

Plump, rust-red chest

Large body, about 8 to 11 inches long

White lower belly

RANGE: Throughout North America in gardens, parks, deciduous woods, tundra, pine forests, golf courses, and farms.

IN AUTUMN, WHEN BERRY CROPS ARE HEAVY, FLOCKS OF HUNDREDS OF CHUCKLING ROBINS WILL FLY IN AND STRIP THE BUSHES OF THEIR BERRIES.

You'll often see plump robins patrolling a lawn, head cocked as if listening for the sound of worms moving through the soil. The robin is actually turning its head to focus an eye on the opening of a worm's tunnel. When it spots a wiggling worm, the robin jabs, tugs, and gobbles it for a meal.

LISTEN FOR: The early morning dawn song of "cheerily, cheerily, cheerio." Robins are one of the first birds to greet the day. Also listen for the Winnie-the-Pooh call of "tut, tut, tut, tut, tut."

NEST SWEET NEST: Robins build deep cup nests of thick mud lined with grasses, plant fibers, and string. They usually lay four beautiful greenish–blue eggs.

Earthworms are a favorite breakfast treat.

NORTHERN MOCKINGBIRD

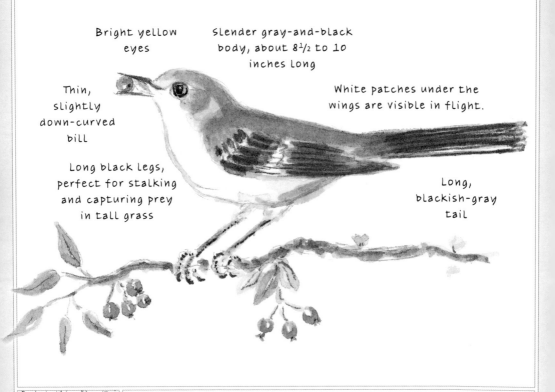

Bright yellow eyes

Slender gray-and-black body, about 8½ to 10 inches long

Thin, slightly down-curved bill

White patches under the wings are visible in flight.

Long black legs, perfect for stalking and capturing prey in tall grass

Long, blackish-gray tail

RANGE: Widespread throughout North America. Found in gardens, parks, deserts, and bushy areas.

THE MIMICKING MOCKINGBIRD IS ALWAYS LEARNING NEW SONGS.

In spring, a male mockingbird may keep you awake all night with his singing, or chase you through the yard and, with a scratching, scolding call, dive at your head. He's warning you that you're in his territory or too close to a nest.

Watch the mocker fall from the sky like a gray leaf and open his white-patched wings with a loud snap. Moths and other insects, frightened by the unexpected movement and color, take flight and are quickly nabbed by the hungry bird.

LISTEN FOR: The mockers mimic hundreds of sounds, from frogs, crickets, dogs barking, cats meowing, to doors squeaking, birds calling, machinery, and more. Try whistling to a mocker, repeating the sound over and over—you'll be surprised by its response.

SECRET SOUND: When a male mockingbird is talking to his mate or to one of his young, he'll perform a quiet "whisper song," which is seldom heard. Be one of the few to hear it.

A young mockingbird waits for lunch.

EASTERN TOWHEE

Bright ruby-red eyes

Black hood

Black upperparts and white underparts (male)

Snowflake-white spot on wing

Rust-red sides

Long tail

Medium-sized body, about 7 to 8¹/₄ inches long

RANGE: Found in thick brush, hedgerows, edges of meadows, farms, parks, and gardens in the eastern United States.

TOWHEES SPEND SO MUCH TIME SCRATCHING AROUND AND NESTING ON THE GROUND THAT THEY'RE OFTEN REFERRED TO AS "GROUND ROBINS." OTHERS CALL THEM "CHEWINKSCHEWINKS."

A flash of rust-red sides, a velvety black hood, a noisy scuffling through leaves, and a command for you to "drink your tea" will let you know that a towhee is in the area.

Towhees spend a lot of time on the ground. Watch how they jump forward and kick leaves and twigs backward, uncovering good snacks like seeds, beetles, larvae, and other insects.

LISTEN FOR: "Drink your tee-e-e-aa, drink your drink your tee-e-e-aa," "chip-chip-chip," "cheewink, cheewink," "three, three, three," "cha-ree, cha-ree," or a trilling "zwee, zwee, zeeeweee."

CHEEPERS PEEPERS: Northern Towhees have bright, ruby-red eyes while Southern Towhees have white eyes.

SPOTTED TOWHEE

Black hood

Orange-red eye

Medium-sized body, about 6½ to 8½ inches long

Thick, pointed, gray-black bill

Black wings spotted and streaked with brilliant white

Cinnamon-red sides, flanks, and undertail

White belly

LISTEN FOR: "Drink teeeaa, drink teeeaa," "drink your tea," and a loud trilling "treeeeeee, treeeeee."

RANGE: Found in chaparral, brushy thickets, edges of meadows and forests, and gardens in the western United States.

CALIFORNIA TOWHEE

Rusty-brown tone around eyes

Plump body, about 8½ to 10 inches long

Short, thick, seed-cracking bill

Dull gray-brown body overall

Face slightly streaked with rust

Long tail

LISTEN FOR: "Pink, pink, pink, pink," a metallic "chink, chink, chink," and "chip, chip, chip," "tseee, tseee, tseee."

RANGE: Found along the west coast of California and Mexico in chaparral, parks, edges of thickets, and gardens.

WHITE-THROATED SPARROW

Touch of yellow between eyes

Strong bill

Pure white throat

Two white wing bars

White-striped crowns (some crowns may be brownish tan)

Plump body, about $6\frac{1}{2}$ to $7\frac{1}{2}$ inches long

Long tail

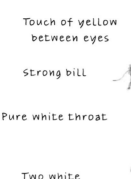

RANGE: The White-throated Sparrow is found more commonly in the East. All three sparrows in this book are found in gardens, parks, bushy hedgerows, dense brush, edges of meadows, overgrown fields, shrubby, weedy areas, and willow thickets.

SPARROWS ARE SECRETIVE, BUT CURIOUS. IF YOU KISS THE BACK OF YOUR HAND, SAY A QUIET "PSSSH, PSSSH, PSSSH," OR MAKE A HIGH SQUEAKING SOUND, THEY'LL OFTEN FLY IN FOR A CLOSER LOOK.

Shy and sociable flocks of sparrows will make short flights away from the cover of sheltering bushes to the dropped seed below your feeder. They'll hop, scratch at the ground, kick at leaves, feed, and, if frightened, fly back into the underbrush in a flash. You'll hear their calls and chattering back and forth, like good neighborhood friends, but you won't easily find their hideouts.

LISTEN FOR: "Old Sam pea, old Sam peabody, peabody, peabody," "seep seep, seep, seep," and "pink, pink."

LOOK FOR: The female White-throated Sparrow may have either white or tan stripes. The ones with white stripes are more aggressive.

This female White-throated Sparrow has white stripes.

SONG SPARROW

Feathers heavily streaked with brown

Long, rounded tail, which it pumps up and down as it flies; whitish underparts, and pinkish legs and feet

Plump medium-sized body, about 5³/₄ to 6³/₄ inches long

"Stickpin" on chest where the streaks meet

LISTEN FOR: This little soprano sings an array of stuttering songs that are different in each region of North America. Some have a repeat stanza of "see, see, bird, see, see, seed, see it" with a trilling buzz at the end. "Ssst, ssst, chip, chip" and "what, what" are some of their other calls. Songs start on a high note and cascade down. The "tik, tik, tik" alarm call lets others know a threat is nearby. A Song Sparrow makes an alarming growl if it's threatened.

WHITE-CROWNED SPARROW

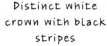

Distinct white crown with black stripes

Plump, medium-sized body, about 6 to 6½ inches long

Pinkish-golden bill

Grayish throat and underparts

White belly, two white wing bars

LISTEN FOR: Although males do most of the singing, females sometimes chime in. The White-crowned Sparrow's whistle is a sad, mournful, up and down trilling "poor, poor, see, see, poor, poor me." Also listen for "chit, chit, chit, chit." These sparrows have different songs throughout North America.

DARK-EYED JUNCO

Brown or dark gray upperparts (females are paler than males)

Dark gray hood

Small and slender body, about 5½ to 6½ inches long

Most have a pinkish bill.

White underparts

Look for the flash of white outer tail feathers when the junco is in flight.

This little junco is fluffed up for warmth.

RANGE: Throughout North America in mixed woodlands, parks, gardens, blueberry fields, pastures, and pine forests.

BIRD-WATCHERS DESCRIBE THE CONTRASTING FEATHERS OF THE NEAT LITTLE JUNCO AS "CLOUDY SKIES OVER SNOWY GROUND."

These small, dark, sparrow-sized birds are so plain they're easy to overlook, even though they may travel in large flocks. In the autumn and winter, you'll find them on the ground below your feeder, picking through seeds like shoppers at a sale. They'll feast on your suet or peanut butter offerings if the feeder is placed in a low, protected area, like on a porch post. They are one of the most common birds in North America.

LISTEN FOR: A long trill repeated over and over. A loud "treeeeeeee, treeeeeee, zeeee, zeee," a stuttered "tea, ee, ee, ee, kew, kew," a "tick tock, tick tock, tick." Sometimes twitters while flying. Males are loud, but when with a female, they sing softly and whistle and trill quietly.

The feather colors and patterns of Dark-eyed Juncos vary throughout the country.

NORTHERN CARDINAL

Large body, about 8½ to 9 inches long

Strong cone-shaped bill

Crest, or tuft of feathers on head

FEMALE
Fawn-brown feathers

Red tip on crest

Black eye

Bright red-orange bill

MALE
Brilliant red feathers

Black eye-mask and chin

Orange-red bill

Long tail

RANGE: Eastern United States, Midwest, Texas, and Arizona. Bushy areas, hedgerows, parks, roadsides, edges of meadows, and gardens.

CHEROKEES BELIEVE THAT THE CARDINAL IS A CHILD OF THE SUN.

You'll probably see the flaming red of the male Northern Cardinal long before you notice his quiet mate. Her fawn-brown feathers help to keep her hidden as she sits on her nest. Cardinals mate for life, and the male is protective and territorial. If you see a big male attacking his reflection in a car mirror or window, he thinks another male is trying to move into his neighborhood.

LISTEN FOR: A happy song of "what cheer, what cheer," "purty, purty, purty, purty," "chew, chew, chew," "here, here, here," or a short, "chip, chip" that sounds like pieces of metal clinking together.

Cardinal tail feather

SPECIAL DELIVERY: Male cardinals bring food for their young, but sometimes they get carried away and bring home too much. What do they do with the extras? They move on to other nests and have been seen feeding baby jays, goldfinches, and even other cardinals.

RED-WINGED BLACKBIRD

Medium-sized body about 6¾ to 9 inches long

Patch of red on each wing, edged in yellow-gold

Rounded wings

Shiny black feathers

Stocky, short tail

RANGE: Found throughout North America in marshes, fields, creekside thickets, and sometimes in drainage culverts with standing water and cattails.

MALE BLACKBIRDS WILL SING LOUDLY, AND REPEATEDLY, PUFF UP, AND FLAUNT THEIR BRILLIANT RED SHOULDER PADS. FEMALES TEND TO GO FOR MALES WITH THE MOST SPUNK AND SPARKLE.

You might think that male Red-winged Blackbirds are the bullies of the neighborhood. During the spring they defend their territories, which can be a full-time job since some males have many mates and nests to protect. After nesting season is over, the birds are more peaceable, and you'll see them bathing and feeding together.

LISTEN FOR: "Seee, seeee, seee, seee," "tear, tear, tear," "pick, pick, pick," "clack-clack," "twink, twink, twink," and the most famous call, "look for meee, look for meee, look for meee." When this last song is sung, the female will often join in for a duet.

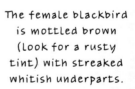

The female blackbird is mottled brown (look for a rusty tint) with streaked whitish underparts.

BALTIMORE ORIOLE

Black head

White wing bar

Medium-sized body, about 6¾ to 7½ inches long

Brilliant orange chest

Orange corners on tail

RANGE: From Canada to the Gulf Coast, and the eastern United States. Found in gardens, orchards, deciduous woods, and streamsides.

ORIOLES WILL EAT FRUIT FROM YOUR FEEDER AND NECTAR FROM HUMMINGBIRD FEEDERS.

The insect-, fruit-, and nectar-eating orioles are like flashes of golden lightning. They're secretive, treetop travelers who feel safest when they're hidden among leaves and branches. Orioles are some of the best nest weavers in the world. They'll carefully build cups, pockets, or pouches of intricately woven fibers that hang beneath palm fronds or leaves. If you see a dazzle of orange feathers or hear a rattling call, watch closely. You may be able to track a bird flying back and forth to its nest.

LISTEN FOR: "Here, here, here, ta here here, here," a whistling song repeated over and over. Often makes a loud, harsh rattle or clattering.

SPECIAL TREATS: Unlike other fruit-eating birds, the Baltimore Oriole prefers the ripest and darkest-colored fruits.

The female Baltimore Oriole is drab with a pale orange breast.

BULLOCK'S ORIOLE

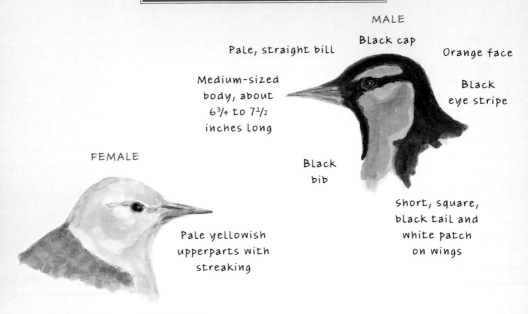

MALE

Black cap

Orange face

Pale, straight bill

Black eye stripe

Medium-sized body, about 6³/₄ to 7¹/₂ inches long

FEMALE

Black bib

Short, square, black tail and white patch on wings

Pale yellowish upperparts with streaking

Yellowish-gray underparts

LISTEN FOR: Chipping, whistles, and nasal barking all mixed together: "chip, chip, you're sweet, you're sweet, you you."

RANGE: Found in deciduous woods, streamsides, orchards, and gardens in the western United States.

HOODED ORIOLE

MALE

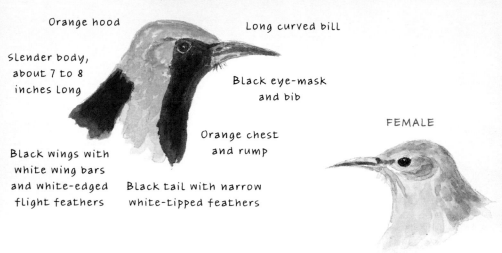

Orange hood

Long curved bill

Slender body, about 7 to 8 inches long

Black eye-mask and bib

FEMALE

Orange chest and rump

Black wings with white wing bars and white-edged flight feathers

Black tail with narrow white-tipped feathers

Olive-yellow-brown on head, rump, and tail

LISTEN FOR: Slurry, rapid, metallic-sounding "veek, veek," "chet, chet, chet," whistles, chatters, and calls imitating other birds.

RANGE: Found in shade trees, streamsides, and palm trees in gardens from the West and Southwest to the Texas Gulf Coast.

HOUSE FINCH

Rust-red markings on the front of its head and chest

Brown cap

Brown-streaked, medium-sized body, about 5½ inches long

Short wings

Notched tail

Female is brown-streaked with whitish underparts.

RANGE: Found in oak woods, deciduous woods, coniferous woods, backyards, scrub, open woodlands, and some urban areas throughout North America. The House Finch is originally a West Coast bird that was illegally sold in pet shops on the East Coast. When set free, they quickly multiplied and settled into their new eastern territory.

DON'T BE SURPRISED TO FIND A HOUSE FINCH NESTING ON A PORCH OR IN A HANGING POT OF PLANTS.

Once the House and Purple Finches discover your feeder, you'll see these birds compete, threaten, and bluff each other. The plucky House Finch will fluff its feathers and lunge at the larger Purple Finch. They'll chatter, scuffle, peck, hop over one another, all in the hopes of eating their fill at your feeder. The House Finch usually wins. What happened to their manners?

LISTEN FOR: The House Finch's call of "chee, chee, chee, chee, chee-wheet, chee-wheet, here, here, here, here" and a slow, scratchy warble, which is often sung by the female when on the nest.

SPECIAL TREATS: Put out a salt block (found in pet stores and bird stores) and finches will flock to it. They also may show up at your hummingbird feeder for a jolt of nectar.

The female House Finch is grayish brown with thick streaks and a gray face.

PURPLE FINCH

Brilliant raspberry-red feathers

Thick conical bill (larger than that of House Finch)

Medium-sized body, about 4³/₄ to 6¹/₄ inches long

Bright rosy rump that flashes in flight

White belly

Notched tail

RANGE: Purple Finches breed in mixed deciduous and coniferous woods. During the winter they go into a variety of habitats, gardens, shrublands, farm fields, forest edges, and parks.

PURPLE FINCHES AVOID VISITING FEEDERS WHERE THEY'RE OUTNUMBERED BY THE FEISTY HOUSE FINCHES.

The brilliantly colored Purple Finch (which is actually raspberry-red) is neater, larger, and chunkier than its House Finch cousin. Watch how the Purple Finch defends its territory at the feeder, even against other Purple Finches. It will raise its head feathers into a crest, which makes it look big and threatening.

LISTEN FOR: The treetop-singing Purple Finch has a higher-toned soprano song performed much more rapidly than the song of a House Finch. They call "cheery, cheery, curlew," "tuck, tuck," and in flight "pit, pit, chip." They often end their jumbled songs with a clear "too-ee, too-ee," like a period at the end of a sentence.

The female Purple Finch has a light, white eye stripe and is coarsely streaked.

PINE SISKIN

Brown streaked body, about 4¼ to 5½ inches long

Slender, pointed bill

Yellow bars on wings

Forked tail with yellow underparts

White underparts with streaking

RANGE: Unpredictable siskins travel in sociable flocks throughout North America in pine forests, mixed woods, parks, weedy fields, and gardens.

ON COLD OR STORMY NIGHTS, PINE SISKINS WILL FLY INTO THICK EVERGREEN BUSHES AND TREES FOR SHELTER.

Pine Siskins are some of the most easily tamed birds you'll find in your garden. If you walk slowly and talk quietly, there is a good chance that they will just eye you warily and continue eating, or, if you offer seed in your hand, they'll sometimes use *you* as a bird feeder. Some are so tame they will even follow you through your yard and into the house!

LISTEN FOR: "ZZZZZZZzeeet," like a zipper opening and closing. Twitters and trills like a canary. Calls "look at me, look at me, look at me, me, me."

FILL 'ER UP: The crop of a Pine Siskin can hold a cargo of seed equaling 10 percent of their body weight.

The female Pine Siskin is streaked with brown.

AMERICAN GOLDFINCH

Bright yellow body, about 4¼ to 5 inches long

Black cap

Cone-shaped yellow bill

Black wings with white markings

In fall and winter, the male and female look alike, with dull olive upperparts, gray wings, and pale yellow underparts, and a male's bill turns gray.

RANGE: Found in flocks throughout North America along fringes of meadows, bushy areas, and gardens.

WATCH HOW THE GOLDFINCH DOES HIS QUICK, ROLLER-COASTER FLIGHT OF UPS AND DOWNS. SOMETIMES THEY LOOK LIKE THEY MIGHT FALL FROM THE SKY.

Fill your feeder with black oil sunflower or black nyjer seed and you'll have a constant flock of twittering, friendly American Goldfinches. They will chatter away until one feels threatened and lets out an alarm call—and like a golden wave, the birds will fly away.

Goldfinches are usually the last birds of the season to build a nest and raise their young. They use the late-season thistle, cattail down, and milkweed to line their nests.

LISTEN FOR: Flocks of goldfinches, unlike most other birds who fly silently, will sing out when flying: "per-chick-oree" and "potato-chip, mee, mee, mee." They twitter and sing like canaries, call "bay-bee, bay-bee" when they're on the nest."

The Lesser Goldfinch has a black cap and dark wings with white wing bars.

EVENING GROSBEAK

Golden-yellow forehead, eyebrow, rump, and chest

Powerful greenish-yellow bill

Stocky brown bird, about 6¼ to 7 inches long

White patches on black wings flash prominently in flight

Short tail

RANGE: Grosbeaks are unpredictable nomads, wandering throughout North America during the winter in mixed woods, conifer forests, suburbs, and mountains in the West.

THE EVENING GROSBEAK IS SOMETIMES MISTAKEN FOR THE AMERICAN GOLDFINCH, WHICH IS SMALLER AND BRIGHTER YELLOW.

These birds are called Evening Grosbeaks because people once believed that they were active and singing only in the evening, but these brilliant birds are out and about all day long. Watch your feeder and you'll see how slowly these big-billed birds move when compared with others. Spend some time with them with seed in your hand; you'll be surprised how easy they are to hand tame. In winter they will visit your salt block (see page 47).

LISTEN FOR: "Clear, clear, clear" and "cleap, clear, cleap." Shrill whistling, chirping, loud calls.

ROAD FOOD: Don't be surprised if you see these birds feeding along roadsides in the winter. They're going after salt crystals, grit, and gravel found on roads.

The female Evening Grosbeak is grayish brown with a green-yellow bill.

YOUR BIRD LIST

Check off the names of birds that visit your feeder.

☐ American Crow

☐ American Goldfinch

☐ American Robin

☐ Anna's Hummingbird

☐ Baltimore Oriole

☐ Black-capped Chickadee

☐ Blue Jay

☐ Bullock's Oriole

☐ California Towhee

☐ Dark-eyed Junco

☐ Downy Woodpecker

☐ Eastern Bluebird

☐ Eastern Towhee

☐ Evening Grosbeak

☐ Hooded Oriole

☐ House Finch

☐ House Wren

☐ Mourning Dove

☐ Northern Cardinal

☐ Northern Flicker

☐ Northern Mockingbird

☐ Pine Siskin

☐ Purple Finch

☐ Red-breasted Nuthatch

☐ Red-winged Blackbird

☐ Ruby-throated Hummingbird

☐ Song Sparrow

☐ Spotted Towhee

☐ Steller's Jay

☐ Tufted Titmouse

☐ Western Bluebird

☐ Western Scrub-Jay

☐ White-crowned Sparrow

☐ White-throated Sparrow

ACKNOWLEDGMENTS

A huge and heartfelt thank you to my brilliant, sensitive, and insightful editor, Ruth Sullivan. You are irreplaceable! Thanks to the "Amaisieing" Maisie Tivnan for her enthusiastic, supportive, and creative input.

Thanks a zillion to Raquel Jaramillo, Orlando Adiao, Carol White, and Susan Jeffers Casel.

Thanks to Peter Workman, who has always believed in me and supported my endeavors. Without the constant involvement and intellect of my husband, Jeff Prostovich, I would still be sitting in my studio, surrounded by a pile of illustrations and bird facts. You made it happen, Jeffrey. Thanks to John "Lefty" Arnold, birder extraordinaire, who has helped me through years of birding and added his three cents' worth to this work.

Faretheewell